The
Innkeeper

JOHN PIPER

ILLUSTRATIONS BY JOHN LAWRENCE

$\mathcal{T}$o Rollin

And All Who Ever Lost

A Child

✳

The Innkeeper

Copyright ©1998 by John Piper

Published by Crossway Books
A division of Good News Publishers
1300 Crescent Street
Wheaton, Ilinois 60187

Illustrations by John Lawrence

Design by Cindy Kiple

First printing, 1998
Printed in the United States of America

LIBRARY OF CONGRESS CATALOGING-IN-PUBLICATION DATA
Piper, John, 1946-
The Innkeeper / John Piper.
p.   cm.
ISBN 1-58134-027-3 (alk. paper)
1. Jesus Christ--Nativity--Poetry.   2. Hotelkeepers-- Bethlehem--Poetry.
3. Christian poetry, American. I. Title. PS3566.I5915   1998
811' .54--dc21
                                                                98-36322
                                                                CIP

So quickly do we pass over the Christmas words, "Herod . . . slew all the male children . . . two years old and under." But the poet lingers, weeping, raging, looking at the dark spot, in hope that any prick of light might become a portal for the sun. And what he sees he strains with words to show—pressing us against the perforation in the wall of pain.

Why this struggle? Why does the poet bind his heart with such a severe discipline of form? Why strain to give shape to suffering? Because Reality has contours. God is who He is, not what we wish or try to make Him be. His Son, Jesus Christ, is the great granite Fact. His hard sacrifice makes it evident that our spontaneity needs Calvary-like discipline. Perhaps the innkeeper paid dearly for housing the Son of God. Should it not be costly to penetrate and portray this pain?

The Innkeeper seeks to reveal the Light that shines behind this brutal moment in history and our own path of suffering.

Come and see!

Jake's wife would have been fifty-eight

The day that Jesus passed the gate

Of Bethlehem, and slowly walked

Toward Jacob's Inn. The people talked

With friends, and children played along

The paths, and Jesus hummed a song,

And smiled at every child he saw.

*H*e paused with one small lass to draw

A camel in the dirt, then said,

"What's this?" The girl bent down her head

To study what the Lord had made.

She smiled, "A camel, sir!" and laid

Her finger on the bulging back

Where merchants bind their leather pack.

"It's got a hump." "Indeed it does,

And who do you believe it was

Who made this camel with his hump?"

Without a thought that this would stump

The rabbi guild and be reviled,

She said, "God did." And Jesus smiled.

"Good eyes, my child. And would that all

Jerusalem within that wall

Of yonder stone could see the signs

Of peace!" He left the lass with lines

Of simple wonder in her face

And slowly went to find the place

Where he was born.

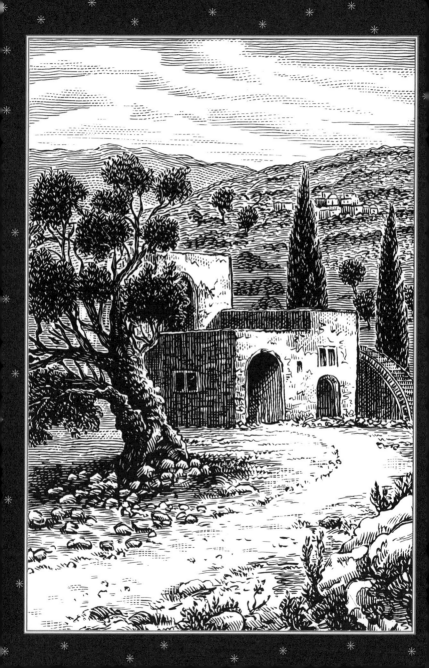

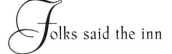olks said the inn

Had never been a place for sin,

For Jacob was a holy man.

And he and Rachel had a plan

To marry, have a child or two,

And serve the folks who traveled through,

Especially the poor who brought

Their meal and turtledoves, and sought

A place to stay near Zion's gate.

They'd rise up early, stay up late,

To help the pilgrims go and come,

And when the place was full, to some,

Especially the poorest, they would say,

"We're sorry there's no room, but stay

Now, if you like, out back. There's lots

Of hay, and we have extra cots

That you can use. There'll be no charge.

The stable isn't very large,

But Noah keeps it safe." He was

A wedding gift to Jake because

The shepherds knew he loved the dog.

"There's nothing in the Decalogue,"

He used to joke, "that says a man

Can't love a dog!"

The children ran

Ahead of Jesus as he strode

Toward Jacob's inn. The stony road

That led up to the inn was deep

With centuries of wear, and steep

At one point just before the door.

The Lord knocked once, then twice, before

He heard an old man's voice, "'Round back!"

It called. So Jesus took the track

That led around the inn.

The old

Man leaned back in his chair and told

The dog to never mind. "Ain't had

No one to tend the door, my lad,

For thirty years. I'm sorry for

The inconvenience to your sore

Feet. The road to Jerusalem

Is hard, ain't it? Don't mind old Shem.

He's harmless like his dad. Won't bite

A Roman soldier in the night.

Sit down." And Jacob waved the stump

Of his right arm. "We're in a slump

Right now. Got lots of time to think

And talk. Come sit and have a drink.

From Jacob's well!" he laughed. "You own

The inn?" the Lord inquired. "On loan,

You'd better say. God owns the inn."

*A*t that the Lord knew they were kin,

And ventured on: "Do you recall

The tax when Caesar said to all

The world that each must be enrolled?"

Old Jacob winced, "Are north winds cold?

Are deserts dry? Do fishes swim

And ravens fly? I do. A grim

And awful year it was for me

When God ordained that strange decree.

How could I such a time forget?

hy do you ask?" "I have a debt

To pay, and I must see how much.

Why do you say that it was such

A grim and awful year?" He raised

The stump of his right arm. "So dazed,

Young man, I didn't know I'd lost

My arm. Do you know what it cost

For me to house the Son of God?"

The old man took his cedar rod

And swept it 'round the place: "Empty.

For thirty years alone, you see?

Old Jacob, poor old Jacob, runs

It with one arm, a dog . . . no sons.

But I had sons . . . once. Joseph was

My firstborn. He was small because

His mother was so sick. When he

Turned three, the Lord was good to me

And Rachel, and our baby Ben

Was born, the very fortnight when

The blessed family arrived.

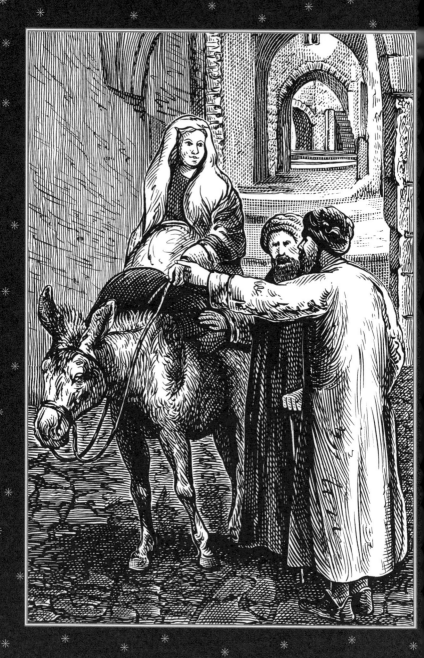

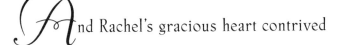

$\mathcal{A}$nd Rachel's gracious heart contrived

A way for them to stay—there in

That very stall. The man was thin

And tired. You look a lot like him."

But Jesus said, "Why was it grim?"

"We got a reputation here

That night. Nothing at all to fear

In that we thought. It was of God.

*B*ut in one year the slaughter squad

From Herod came. And where do you

Suppose they started? Not a clue!

We didn't have a clue what they

Had come to do. No time to pray,

No time to run, no time to get

Poor Joseph off the street and let

Him say good-bye to Ben or me

Or Rachel. Only time to see

lifted spear smash through his spine

And chest. He stumbled to the sign

That welcomed strangers to the place,

And looked with panic at my face,

As if to ask what he had done.

Young man, you ever lost a son?"

The tears streamed down the Savior's cheek,

He shook his head, but couldn't speak.

"Before I found the breath to scream

I heard the words, a horrid dream:

'Kill every child who's two or less.

Spare not for aught, nor make excess.

Let this one be the oldest here,

And if you count your own life dear,

Let none escape.' I had no sword,

No weapons in my house, but Lord,

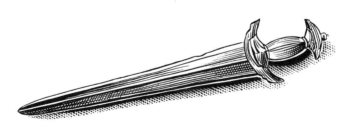

I had my hands, and I would save

The son of my right hand. . . .So brave,

O Rachel was so brave! Her hands

Were like a thousand iron bands

Around the boy. She wouldn't let

Him go, and so her own back met

With every thrust and blow. I lost

My arm, my wife, my sons—the cost

For housing the Messiah here.

Why would he simply disappear

And never come to help?" They sat

In silence. Jacob wondered at

The stranger's tears.

"I am the boy

That Herod wanted to destroy.

You gave my parents room to give

Me life, and then God let me live,

And took your wife. Ask me not why

The one should live, another die.

God's ways are high, and you will know

In time. But I have come to show

You what the Lord prepared the night

you made a place for heaven's Light.

In two weeks they will crucify

My flesh. But mark this, Jacob, I

Will rise in three days from the dead,

And place my foot upon the head

Of him who has the power of death,

And I will raise with life and breath

Your wife and Ben and Joseph too,

And give them, Jacob, back to you

With everything the world can store,

And you will reign forever more."

✳   ✳   ✳